In loving memory of my mother

THIS JOURNEY BELOVED HAS NO BEGINNING AND NO END

IT IS A SPIRAL DANCE THROUGH THE WAVES OF LIFE

GUIDING YOU INTO LIVING AND LOVING WITH YOUR
HEART OPEN

A JOURNEY OF REMEMBERING YOUR CONNECTION TO THE
EARTH

A REAWAKENING OF YOUR INNER WISDOM

MAY YOU THROUGH THIS JOURNEY INTO YOURSELF
BECOME A VESSEL FOR THE HOLY LIGHT OF YOUR SPIRIT

MAY YOU FIND THE LIGHT IN THE DARKEST PLACES AND
TRANSFORM THEM INTO LOVE

RETURNING TO THE GREAT MOTHER OF US ALL

DISSOLVES ALL WOUNDS OF SEPARATION

WE WALK IN SPIRALS AND SIT IN CIRCLES

TO REMEMBER WE ARE ONE

Return to the Mother

A Spiral Journey of Descent into the Great Mother's Womb

By Rebecca Wilson

www.rebecca-wilson.com

Return to the Mother

ISBN: 978-1-8383428-0-7

Artwork by @seedsofspells and Jessie White

For more information about the author, Rebecca Wilson, or for additional trainings, speaking engagements, or media enquiries, please visit:

www.rebecca-wilson.com

I am not here to save you
I AM here to show you
All the parts of you
You have forgotten along the way
I am here to guide you
Back into the truth of your soul
I am here to guide you
Down into the wisdom of your womb
I am here to hold you
In the deepest love ever known
I am here to show you
All the parts of yourself you don't yet see
All the magic within you
All the beauty waiting to be birthed from you
I am here for you sister
I am here with you
Walk with me

The End

Healing

Sometimes feels like dying

In truth it is

Aspects of the self

That no longer serve

Releasing

In the surrender

The letting go

The Death

Becomes A Birth

Women in a circle

Opening sacred directions

Sharing mantra to our divine mother

Thank her for holding us

For Carrying us through

As we collectively enter into a place

of inner sanctuary

In Connection to our eternal worlds

The mind slowly drifts away

we are resting here fully embodied

To feel

To move

To dance

To shake

To be still

To explore

To express

To experience

Our divinity within

To let go

To clear

To release

To cut ourselves free

From the lies we have been told

That we are too much

We have never been too much

We have never been not enough

We have always been

Just as we are

The divine expressing herself through us

In many ways

In many shapes

In many forms

We sit in circle

All as teachers

We sit in circle

All as students

We sit in circle

To remember

We sit in circle

As One

Becoming

In The Unbecoming

The intensity of life
Crashes against you

With a knowing
There is nowhere to hide

Can you allow life to
Break you open

Crack you open
Layer by layer

Until there is no veil remaining

The Heart

The heart

An instrument

For the song of Love

The beautifully terrifying song of grief

The earth-shattering song of sadness

The universe exploding song of love

The cosmic awakening of soul upon soul connection

The divine meeting the divine

Through the song of the heart

The Collective Heart

Is Shaking

The Collective Heart

Is Breaking

Seasons and Cycles

Replaying

Patterns and Thoughts

Reframing

The Collective Stories Rising

A Great Time of Reweaving

Tapestry's of A New Age

Through The Collective Release

The Individual Heart Grieves

A Pouring Out if The Pain

To Open into Love

The Shaking of The Roots

Re Rooting into Truth

Revealing The Heart's Great Awakening

To the heart that cracks open

Arriving in boundless form

The Heart that shatters into a million pieces

Arriving into an infinite vast space of oneness

The heart that loves with no limitations

The heart that loves with no conditions

The heart that opens into an eternal loving embrace

The heart that arrives into Love

A love that has no boundaries

A love that knows not of separation

A love that knows not of abandonment or rejection

The heart that melts into liquid love of the divine

The sweet tender heart that opens like a flower in bloom

The heart that wishes to love with no limitations

The heart that opens into a deep pool of infinite bliss

The heart

The heart that's fully opened

A Woman Who Loves Changes The World

A Woman who loves her pain

A Woman who loves her fear

A Woman who loves her flaws

A Woman who love her anger

A Woman who loves her joy

A Woman who loves her body

A Woman who loves her wildness

A Woman who loves her inner child

A Woman who loves her own feminine

A Woman who loves her own masculine

A Woman who loves her rage

A Woman who loves her passion

A Woman who loves her story

A Woman who loves her grief

A Woman who loves her sorrow

A Woman who loves her light

A Woman who loves her magic

A Woman who loves her natural state of being

A Woman who loves all of her Emotions

A Woman who loves ALL parts of HERSELF will change the World

There is no end to the depth of the heart

A vast limitless space

A void

Only when you enter into the spiral dance of this endless space

Will you begin to know love

Following the heart

Confirming the heart deep in The Womb

Dropping deep into the vast limitless space of the heart

Arriving at a void

A never ending vortex of possibility

A never ending spiral of energy

The heart cracks open

Breaks

Shatters

All illusions vanish

Nothing can be heard

Nothing but the heart

Only the heart's voice

Asking me to drop deeper

To surrender

Down into her

To plant the opening as an offering down into my womb space

To confirm at the heart womb
That which only the body knows

Once the heart is this open
Only she can lead

The mind retires
In humility
To the heart's desires

The heart's path is calling
Only the heart can answer the call

At first not all the heart asks makes sense
The mind trying to question that which the heart feels

Descending the heart to the void within the womb
All knowing and wisdom can be found here
Surrender deeper to the heart's calling
Only the heart open to infinite love can lead the way
Ask no questions of the mind
Only feel the heart's feelings

As the Heart Bud Blooms into Her Full Flower

She Awakens a ReMembering

Waves of Ecstasy

Limitless Bliss

The Heart That Fully Opens

Knows Pain

Knows Suffering

The Heart That Fully Surrenders

Knows Loss

Knows Grief

The Heart That Fully Opens

Feels Tenderness

Feels the Rawness

The Heart That Fully Loves

Has Sat Within The Shadows

The Heart That Fully Opens

Cracks into All There is To Be Felt

This Heart Knows The Power of
Allowing itself to BREAK OPEN

OVER and OVER AGAIN

Courage Lives Within This Heart
That Allows Itself To Bloom
Even When It Feels like Closing

Reflections of The Heart

What if you just let go
Let go of all the holding on
Let go of all the walls

What if you just surrendered
Surrender to the waves of emotions passing through your chest

What if you allowed
Allowed yourself to feel
Allowed yourself to express it all

What would the Heart say
If she had freedom to share her voice

How fully could she open
How fully could she love

What would she feel like if she had no walls or barriers

How would she express the waves of emotion that pass through her

Could she love others more openly

Could she hold others more deeply

Could she allow the divine grace of love to shine her light through her

How would the Heart feel without any fear or limitations of the mind...

Arriving into the vast space of the limitless heart

Taken deep into the spirals of her embrace

A small voice speaks to me

Let go

An ancient part that still holds on

To the illusion of control

A part that has feared to release all holding
All grasping

A part that fears not knowing

I speak to her with Love and tell her
It is ok now
We can let go
There isn't anything to be afraid of

Ahhhh she sighs

Thank you

And I Fall down into the Vast Void of my Limitless Heart

Thank you she whispers again

I can now open up to a deeper love

Love is the Letting Go of All Control

Surrender into love's embrace

It is your time to receive

Let the doors open and let love pour in

Surrendering into Her Embrace

She holds the back of my body
As I sink down into her embrace

Her soft strong presence
Allowing my body to melt

Her roots growing up within me
My energy melting into her

We begin to dance as one
Move as one
Breathe as one

Her loving embrace grows deeper
As I fully surrender to her call

Let go she whispers to me
Allow yourself to let go...
I release all control
I offer myself to her

The primal waves of Shakti
Begin to rise within me
Spiral through me
Course around me
Radiate beyond me

Legs shaking
Pelvis rocking
Spine undulating
Heart breaking
Open

She is taking me
In to her
Down into her Womb

Showing me the depth of her love
Surrender my child
Let go

Allow yourself to be born again from the loving depths of my womb

You are a child of this Earth

It is your time to return to
Your Original Innocence

It is Your Time To Return To Love

Reaching into the depth of the heart

A vast open infinite space

Swirling round and down

Into the velvet darkness

Soft space with no edges

Dissolving

Into the nothingness that is everything

The waves of energy

Spiralling down into the womb

As the river of love flows

Heart to Womb

Womb to Heart

Vast Spaciousness arrives

Infinite expansion awaits....

The spirals

The waves

The emotions

Rising up to the surface

Asking to be felt

Longing to be known

Desperate to be seen

The tightening of your chest

The beating of your heart

The remains of the aches

The cages you have placed there to keep you small and safe

Summoning the courage to feel

Trusting the fire will come

Surrendering to let go

The knot in your stomach

The twists within your spine

The ball locked in your throat

The deep pain within your womb

The growl deep within

Of a voice of primal sounds

The parts of you silenced

Through the suppression of anger and rage

Welcoming all parts you

That you have ignored and cast aside

Calling back your power

The fragments of your soul

To begin once again to feel the pulsating love in your heart beat

The love that is Running through your veins

To remember you are a Child Of Love

You are walking the journey home

As a living expression of nature

We Are

Moved

Pulled

Twisted

And

Turned

By the tides of her

Her seasons

Her cycles

Her flow

In flux and flow

Planets move and dance around the sun

Moon shines full

And rests in the Void

We are all reflections of the manifestations within the universe

Allowance

Allowing

The waves of sadness

The feeling of heaviness

The rise of joy

The feeling of bliss

The turns and tides of the waves of life

To be human as a reflection of nature

The awakening of the feminine nature

An explosion of the heart

The unfolding of a flower in bloom

The expression of joy

The feeling of a song moving within the cells

of the body

This opening to pleasure requires an expansion of the heart

A deep surrender to the waves of ecstasy
of life

Am allowing of life to love through you

A constant opening of the heart's petals

The Womb

This journey of the womb is an

UnWeaving of stories

UnPeeling of layers

UnShackling of hidden wisdom

UnEarthing of your Primordial way

UnVeiling of all the illusions that have kept you from this Holy Relationship

With Yourself.

This is a journey of

Wild

Innocent

Primordial

Raw

Nakedness

As you awaken the energetic grid lines of your body

You return to your Holy Self

When we take the journey back into Connection with our earth mother and the sacred land of our bodies we are teaching ourselves that separation is an illusion, a wounding and does not need to be our reality

We ReMember through this sacred union of Earth and Spirit
Body and Soul

That we are wired for togetherness not separation

That this is the Holy Grail

Womb Earth Connection

As we open to Her

We open up to ourselves

Feminine Path of Awakening

When awakening to the path of the feminine we are taking a cyclical journey
There may be a feeling at times that we are spinning in circles

This is exactly what we are doing
We are returning to the spiral of creation
Spiralling with the circles of life
Unwrapping
Unravelling
Unpeeling
The layers of linear projection and conditions that have kept you bound

A journey into the portal of your womb
To remember

Everything you desire already lives within you
Waiting to be Birthed

When a woman becomes conditioned,
denies or holds distorted imprints around her
Primal Life Force

She Disconnects from her Ability to Co-Create with the universal womb
consciousness of Manifestation & Creation

As we take moments to sit quietly, gently holding our sacred womb space in our hands we settle and breathe into connections with Mother Earth

From this space we are able to ask her for her guidance, for her to support us to UnSpiral years of layers and imprints.

This is a non-logical process
It is to be felt
Within and From the Depths of your soul

Dropping into this sacred centre opens up hidden feelings, this can be scary, overwhelming and awakening with a feeling of traveling in time

Feelings of fear, shame, panic, grief, pain may rise up from years of suppression yet it is in the welcoming of these feeling sensations that we are able to clear and heal...

As these deep feelings rise up they begin to dissolve the masks and layers bound around us that have been placed there to keep us "safe"

It is from this space of opening up to it all that we can be met once again by the Pure Love Within us infused by the pristine innocence of our primal nature.

A renewed sense of life arises

As we welcome ourselves to be reborn into the unconditional love of our

Original Mother

As we take a journey to Awaken the ancient Feminine Wisdom Within we awaken the inner light of creation

This light may have been shut down, dimmed or not allowed - all actions of fear of shining bright in the world.
Rooted in a deep fear of being seen.

When we awaken Feminine Wisdom we awaken light energy within our body temple, we awaken to deeper levels of intimacy and open up to allow ourselves to be fully seen in our full shining light...

This allows you step into your full light and power.. supporting you to share your gifts, healing, voice and unique medicine with the world...

The powerful wisdom of your life experiences are your souls reason for being here
This requires courage, trust and a clear connection to your womb space.
To stand in your full Heart Womb Power and share your visions and creations with the world...

Knowing that the Earth needs your beauty, wisdom and light to shine in your fullness

Sacred Lands of The Body

Welcoming all parts of yourself back home to your body is a journey of remembering all the parts of yourself once denied, shut down, pushed away, abandoned, rejected or those parts that took flight through trauma, pains and upset.

Living in a society that praises the upward moving energy of the Masculine has us disconnected from the downward moving energy of the feminine.

Through conditions to rise up, climb up, pick yourself up we are in a thought form that descending back into our emotions, feelings of our bodies is something to be seen as wrong, unsuccessful.

When we Journey back into sacredness of the land of our bodies, we are also reconnecting and recommunicating with the land of Mother Earth.

We become one with the seasons and cycles both within us and outside of us too, we establish a relationship with the nature of our inner landscape and the landscape of the Mother too. As we embrace her in all her many layers and elements we too learn how to embrace ourselves and the emotions that express themselves throughout us.

Primordial Womb

When we rest in the primordial depth of our Womb we are resting in the Eternal embrace of the Mother.

A profound inner silence arrives, peaceful and so so potent.

We are in a state of gestation... still, quiet growing...

We are literally gestating within timelessness, the birthless and deathless state, the Shamanic realms

When we drop onto the peace of our pelvis and the depths of our womb spaces we are entering a state of inner gestation which is to tap into deep rest within Self.

We are replenished at every level
We know the deep velvety silence of our inner temple.

All sense of struggle ceases as we rest in Connection to our inner Truth.
With deep breaths allow yourself to relax your awareness into the space of your womb.

Breathe deeply.
Breathe deeply.
Breathe deeply.

Allow your awareness to drop deeper, deeper, deeper over these next few
breaths, until you find your awareness easily relaxing through the portal of your
womb into the primordial womb.

Rest here in this deep wide, vast open space

Feel the quiet
Hear the silence

Allowing yourself to feel landed in your womb's eternal state of being

Take a few breaths here, allowing your whole body and womb to be
replenished.
Then, breath your heart down
Into open up into your womb like a flower.

Journeying The Cosmos of The Body

The body is a universe all in herself
When grounded and rooted we enter the cosmos of the mothers body through
the activated star points in the soles of our feet
Anchored into the cosmic womb web of the earth's energy grids
Our Feminine crown - root, pelvis & womb - awaken To all the wisdom within
the earth plane of our bodies and the body of Mother Earth.
This rooted activation awakens the celestial star point at the crown of our head,
our masculine crown activates and connects up to the cosmic womb of the sky.

Stars fall from the sky and land upon the sacred land of our bodies as we
Journey deep into the roots of our cosmos within

Awakening our life force through the feminine realms of our pelvis, Womb, legs
and feet we are able to access heaven through the earth to fully embody the
cosmic womb consciousness

When a woman is rooted with a deep sense of safety, belonging within herself and her connection to Mother Earth her heart and cervix can relax open

The heart and cervix have their own energetic pathways of connection which open in safety and love.

The cervical gateway is a bridge between the world opens and dilates when in conscious connection to the Heart.

This opening allows us to surrender all control and fall into the vast cosmic landscape of Earth consciousness - her universal embodied love.

She never stops opening and giving to us. As we surrender into her embrace she supports us to continuously move towards a greater awakening of the multidimensional beauty of our internal landscape.

Womb Lineage

Ancestral Line

Women of the Blood Line

The Sacred flow of the Holy Blood

The blood that creates all life on earth

Each womb within the lineage

Birthing from the menstrual line

The holy blood

The red thread

Passed down through generations

All wombs connected

By the holy thread of all life

Weaving dreams

As we weave dreams into our womb consciousness we begin to change the
tapestry of our womb energy, body and mind energies. This shift changes the
coded geometry with in our energy field, this shift then naturally changes the
internal vibration of our womb space... the portal of all creation. This shift
creates a new place, a new space and new blueprint from which to manifest,
create, gestate, and birth new experiences into our reality.

Divine Mother's Womb

The great mother's cosmic womb

Her heavenly womb of light

The great mothers earth womb

Her grounded womb of love

When we take a journey of remembering that we are a child of the light and children of the earth we awaken to the knowing that our beloved divine mother is our great mother

Our source of all life

Beyond the physical experience of birthing into life through our birth mother's womb

We release the veil and illusion of separation

We remember we are not and never have been separated or abandoned

That we are children born from the great mother's womb

Where all beings are birthed from

One great womb of light

Where no separation exists

The illusions dissolve into a vast ocean of love

A returning to our divine mother's womb

Here we rest within her loving embrace

Returning To The Mother's Womb

When we take a journey of returning

Into the great mother's Womb

We meet a space of remembering

We are everything

Everything is us

We remember all separation is an illusion

And return to oneness with all of life

We need not worry or fear abandonment

As there is nothing to leave us

We are all

We need not push away or deny love

As there is nothing to push away

We remember we are love

All wounds fear and anxieties

All disconnection and aloneness

Dissolve into her womb's embrace

We return to wholeness
As a child of the universe
A child of the earth

We remember all parts of us are sacred
The veil of separation dissolves into loving womb of our great mother

Here we remember her love is eternal
We remember ourselves as one

Awakening Earth Consciousness through The Womb Portal

We each are a child of Mother Earth
Yet through time we have lost our earth connecting ways of life

Mother Earth calls you now to remember and reconnect to her through the Earth
Gateways into her Crystalline Grids of Her Womb Of Creation

We journey into the roots of your body re awakening a profound connection to
the earth of your body and Mother Earth herself

Arriving at the earth gateway of your womb space
Awakening the earth portals of Creation

Remembering

When Rooted We Rise

With Strong Roots We Create Safety Within Our Inner Womb Temple

When Grounded We Birth Visions Upon Earth

When we activate our earth-bound energy through our body we walk a path of awakening to Earth Consciousness

Rooted
Grounded
Earth Connection

Opening a pathway of connection between you and Mother Earth

Arriving into the womb of the earth

You are able to receive her love, support, ancient wisdom and knowledge

A feeling a safety and healing arrives as you remember you are a child of the earth

We harmonise with the primal pulse of the earths womb as a song of our hearts

Reclaiming our place and life on Earth

Rise of Shakti

Descent of Grace

Primal wild shakti rising
Awakening root to crown

Spiralling
Swirling
Circling

Shakti rises through the blocks and distortions held locked in the body

A rising of yourself
Your primal nature

Into A release of limitations

Unbound
She washes through you

Leaving no wound unearthed

Ascending into the crown
Awakening codes of god

The rise is her release

Opening to a channel of pure divine light

The light of grace descending

Pouring down
Codes of light

Root

Shaking

Opening

Releasing

In times of great change our foundations can often feel like they are shaking beneath us

Our roots breaking away from the old landscape of our life narrative

These Roots woven, Spiralled deeply into the foundations of our earth

Our earth being the narratives and patterns we play or have played into over time

The longer the story the deeper the root

As our roots shake we begin to experience a breaking free of all traumas and life experiences that have been stored there

Our roots hold our primitive nature of survival, safety and security

Old memories, experiences and emotions are stored in the root, the woven tapestry of past experiences of pain, fear, lack of safety often rise up to the surface as this shaking arrives into our lives

As we currently find ourselves in a collective root shaking, there may be an uprising of unexpressed root memories, emotions and feelings

May we hold the knowing that this shaking up is all part of a reweaving of a great tapestry of life

As we experience this great Collective and
Personal root shake may we hold gently the wisdom that we are shaking free from the
Old roots and the old ways to plant new roots and new ways

Shake free the roots from the old

Plant new seeds for the new roots

Awakening Spirals of Creation

When the scared portals of the cosmos and the earth meet in union a powerful energy ignites.

All meets in the fertile ground of matter, birthed from the starlight of womb consciousness, manifesting new ideas, dreams and visions into the world.

It is from this grounded place of connection to the earth that we are able to drawn down from the cosmic realms inspiration, divine gifts, messages from spirit into our womb spaces to be gestated and birthed into the physical earth plane.

If this grounded energy is not present these dreams and visions will stay floating within the cosmos, spiralling within the mind and third eye centre, unable to be pulled down into the physical realm due to lack of connection to the physical body, world and matter.

The Descent

Close your eyes

Breathe deeply

See in front of your eyes

And expansive space of darkness

Surrounding you

No light

No stars

No moon

Nothing but vast darkness

Across the horizon into infinity

Allow yourself to stay open

Do not contract in fear

Do not turn away

Hand over yourself to the darkness

The black shimmering void

Do not hold hope of light

Do not try to change

Surrender fully

Completely

Allow yourself to merge with the void and the mystery of life

In the Fertile Darkness of our Wombs

There is a lot to be felt

A deep place to connect

A sacred place we touch

A sweetness we can taste

In the quietness we hear so much

It is within the darkness that

Our senses awaken....

Honouring your journey back home into the vast velvet space of your Sacred
Centre

As we arrive into the depths of our Earth Womb to let everything go and trust
the cycles of Nature

The Void

The space of velvet darkness

Submerged in sweet soft tender embrace

Allowing the body and mind to release into this space of being held

Within the unknown

The pain is held within the holding

The beauty is experienced within the letting go

Down into the waves of nothingness

The Portals Open

WOMAN

The bridge between the worlds

The Holy Vessel
The Holy Temple
The Holy Grail

WOMAN

Portals opening to the great cosmic womb

The great womb of inspiration, conception, communication

The Heart A Portal
The Womb A Portal
The Voice A Portal
Spoken Words A Portal
She Is The Portal

Opening

Expanding

Receiving

Receiving light codes of Creation

Her life

Her love

Her art

Her inspiration

Her conception

Of all her soul calls to conceive from higher realms down into the earthly

realms

Her womb

Expansive

Open

Receptive

Ready

Fertile space for the seeds of Creation

Plant

Root

Grow

Gestating

Growing

Nourishing

Nurturing

Nature in her cycles

The Great Earth womb

The gateway to the earth

Activated

Opened

The portal earth gate

Ready to birth the seeds of inspiration, creation and conception

WOMAN the birther of all life

WOMAN the vessel for the divine

WOMBAN The Holy Temple

WOMBAN The bridge between heaven and earth

Cervical Awakening

Surrendering into the Unknown

Falling

Down

Sinking

Down into the void

Dying into The Darkness

Floating

Surrendering

Releasing into the black velvet embrace

Submerged into a void of luminous black light

Awakening

Awakening

Sinking

Into a field of shining stars

Waves

Pulsating

Waves

Of ecstasy

Primal erotic bliss

Heart exploding

Opening

Waves of Grief

Pulsing

Shaking

Shaking

Screaming

Kaleidoscope colours

Creating

Patterns of cosmic realms

Softening

Softening

Softening

Releasing

Surrendering

Deeper

Deeper

Down

Down

Into the Abys

Dissolving

Melting

Releasing all control

Given fully

Holy

To the darkness within

Opening
Opening

To the beloved arms of God

The Yearning

Feels Like Dying

Heart Breaking
Great Expansion

Awakening into The Depth
Of The Heart's Longing

Dying Into The Arms Of God

~ A Dissolving into Love

In The Shadows of Your Deepest Fears Hides Your Greatest Light

It is when we allow ourselves to feel the

Great Grief of the heart that we liberate ourselves into Love

The Gateway of Birth + Death

We Are in The Great Cervical Awakening

Passing Through the Tunnel of Darkness

With No Sight of Light

We Give Ourselves Fully

To The Waves

Surrendering Fully

Placing Down The Armour

The Heart Cracking

Breaking Open into Grief

Pouring Out a Release

~ An Opening To Love

And one day

All the dark heavy grief

That has lived in the

Depth of the Heart

Opens

And is felt

As the greatest

Expansion of Love

~ Grief is present because Love lives here

The earthbound descent

Primal awakening

The physical form opening to the earth below

Womb

Cervix

Birth canal

Yoni

Opening

Just as the chrysalis within the cocoon

Grows and expands

Beyond the size

Ready to birth into the world

As the butterfly

Baby has grown and filled the womb

Is ready to birth too

The growth and transformation of the birth process a journey of baby and parents

Shifting

Moving

Changing

Growing

Shedding

Birth requires a release to welcome the new

Descending down

Into the crimson red flow

Primal power taking me
Down into the void

Where the black light of consciousness
Transforms into a red river

Flowing waves of sacred blood
I am floating within

Releasing into an ocean of darkness
Surrendering all control

Held safe within the tidal waves of Creation

The waves of death and release

Welcoming in time a new cycle of beginnings
But for now the crimson red waves take me

Into the absolute unknown

And I will allow myself to taken

In full surrender to the flow

Touching Your Deepest Pain

When patterns and pains persist

It is because My beloved

You haven't touched them deep enough

You haven't sunk into the core of them

You haven't allowed them

You haven't given yourself fully

To the grief

To the sadness

To the betrayal

To the anger
To the rage

To the pain point inside you

There is more to give

A death

A release

A dissolving

Only when we die to the darkness

Can we welcome the light

Only when we give ourselves FULLY to Grief

Can we open to Love

Grace is waiting to descend upon you

As a beloved child of God

This is your birth right

Holy child of the light

But first the holy grail

Of descent

Into the Darkness

All the way

To be born into the light

Womban

Your menstrual blood is sacred

You are cyclical in nature

You are nature

Moving in cycles

Changing shape and form

You are not meant to stay the same forever

You are meant to wax and wane

Like the moon in the sky

You are allowed to fluctuate

You are allowed to expand

You are allowed to contract

Give yourself permission to let go

Of the linear way of living

Allow yourself to exhale a deep sigh of relief

As you remember your body is sacred

And you are Nature

Pelvic Crown

Pelvic Crown
Royal Throne

The pelvis and root is the Feminine crown holding the womb
This portal opens up to the wisdom of the earth and the doorways to heaven
upon earth.

This is the portal to the sensual embodiment of cosmic wisdom here on Earth.

This portal opens us up to the magical realms of life upon earth, awakening a
grounded expression of awakened energy, supporting a rooted connection to
celestial energies and primordial Shakti.

Fully embodied, Alive, rooted, sensual, activated primordial Connection to
Earth's core.

This awakens an ecstatic joy to be here on Earth in a physical body.
Restoring ancient templates of wisdom

A golden template of the divine

Ancient codes of Queen energy

Placed upon the throne of the pelvic crown

Blood Wisdom

Your menstrual blood holds deep ancient wisdom

The lineage of your blood line

The roots of your lineage

The magical ancient ways of the feminine

Deep within your cells

As a woman sheds her womb lining
She is remembering
She is letting go
She is evolving
She is releasing
She is dropping within her infinite wisdom

To listen to the wisdom of her blood
Women during their bleed are the most connected to source and spirit

There roots open to the wisdom of the Earth

A pure open channel for the divine

Resting at the time of your bleed is a profound way to tune into the wisdom she has to offer you

This is a time to reconnect to the lost Feminine Arts of ritual and ceremony

Descending into The Black Light of
The Cosmic Womb

The Space of All Creation

When we descend into the pure innocence of our primordial womb space we
access the black light of womb consciousness

This black light holds the codes of creation
It is from this space that we are able to embody the primal energy of Shakti.

The Black light is the essence of the divine feminine.

A hidden, rich, nourishing light within us that we can dive into in order to come
back to ourselves, our purest essence of innocence.

All matter is birthed from a black void within the cosmos
This is the Birth Point of Shooting Stars and Light

Take a deep breath

Let your body know

She is safe

Safe to open

To feel and to let go

There will arrive a time upon your spiral path of inner awakening that you begin to feel yourself break

A cracking open

Your heart
Your mind
Your body
Your beliefs
Your limitations
The illusions you have told yourself
The illusions the world has told you

You will find yourself cracked wide open
To meet your raw, wild, vulnerable heart
Beating in your chest
A song you have never heard before

You will find yourself stripped back to your core
Naked in your vulnerability
Nothing or nowhere to hide

You will from a placed deeper than you thought possible find your strength
A strength that is so very soft
Fragile
New

An innocence birthing from your purest heart

My prayer for you is that you allow yourself to meet this place within you dear
sister

That you give yourself permission to Journey into the deepest darkest parts of
your heart
To rip out the illusions

And leave nothing but the Love of The Divine within the cage of your chest

Let love be Alive Within you
Allow grace to fall upon you

My prayer for you
Let Love Guide You

Let Love Be You

Womb World

As you close your eyes and descend down into the dark vast space of your womb

You meet a magical door way

A door way to your Womb World

A door way of all possibilities

Awakening Womb World
YOU ARE invited you on a journey into the magical world of your womb

A mythical story woven through a journey of liminal time awaits you

An ancient remembering of the wisdom within her cyclical nature as the nature of all

A magical fairy-tale landscape awakens as you step through the doorway into your womb world

The opening of the birth canal

An opening of expression
An opening to life
An opening to birth
An opening to death
The expression of life birthing

Down through the birthing channel
From darkness into the light

The birthing of the baby
The birth of the mother

The death of what was

The release of all that is no more
To open into the new

Mother

The rite of passage
As baby journeys into the earth world

Awakening Primal Shakti

Waves of ecstasy

Ripples of energy

Pulsations of power

Spiralling
Swirling
Vibrating

Arriving down into the primal seat of the tail bone

This ancient bone of primal power

Animal nature

The seat where once the tail extended down into connection to the earth

The tailbone
The antenna to the wisdom spoken from Mother Earth

This is the seat of primal intuition

Animal impulse
Primordial nature

The sacred space of Shakti

Coiled within the root of the body

The divine rises
From root to crown

The divine descends
From crown to root

Tingles in the tailbone

Awakening a long forgotten primitive nature
A nature of connection to all existence
A primal nature of holiness

The seat
The throne
Of the holy Shakti

Orgasm and Birth

Mirror the reflection

Of the

Expansion and Contraction

Of the Universe

Inner Listening

To the Sweet Sound of the Body, Heart and Spirit Guiding the way

To the parts that are calling for love and attention

To the parts that are no longer required and the death of those outdated layers

To Awaken To The Process of Transformation

By Listening not Pushing

Releasing The Push to Soften into Listening

The contraction arrives
Deep waves of tightening

An impulse to push
To resist the pain
To resist the closing

Yet in the space a welcoming
A welcoming of inner listening

What arises within the contraction
What arises within the push
What arises within the "pain"

Uncomfortableness?
Inability to surrender?
Control?
Grasping?
Holding on?

This is the reflective experience of

Our current collective experience

The rebirth of ourselves

The birth of life

All is found within the contraction and expansion

The fluctuations of

Shadow and Light

Yet do we really need to push?

Where does the energy behind the push originally manifest from?

Fear?

A need to just get through the process at play?

What if....

We as individuals

We as a collective

We as mothers

We as the birthers

We are the ones who are re birthing ourselves

The Mother is Shaking

The Divine Feminine is Rising

She is releasing the Wounded Masculine

Wounds Woven into systems

Systems that are built within our collective external and personal internal landscape

The eradication of the passive feminine / mother

The release of the False Light is Now

This clearing
Makes way for the Fire Feminine to Rise

The Fierce Love of the Mother

The commitment to Seeing all parts of the self

The fierce love of the Mother you are unable to hide from

She will show you yourself

She will show all ways your inner masculine is wounded and part of the internalised and externalised systems

This time is that of meeting the Mother Within

To ReMother Yourself with Fierce Love

The Love of Truth
The Love of Real Light

Mothering **yourself means** meeting your emotional, physical, and spiritual needs

As your adult self now

It is Time To Mature into Accountability

It is Time To Love Yourself Enough to See Your Shadows

It is Time to Awaken the Alchemist Within

Transmute your Pain into The Power of Love

In This Time

You Can No Longer Hide

The Mother Sees All

The Mother Within You
She Sees and she WILL NOT let you hide

She will arrive as uncomfortable feelings, thoughts and insights
She asks you to love them into the light

She will show you new ways to see, she will show you all the places you haven't
yet seen

Don't Turn Away

Turn towards yourself with Love

Root Breathing

Drawing the breath down into the
Roots supports a softening, opening and expanding into connection with the
earth.

The earth Gateway of the womb is the gateway of birth.

Birth of new life
Birth of Creations
Birth of yourself

The Root Is Where it All Begins

Root of Matter

Roots of Bloodline

The first space to develop during our gestational time is our root

The Perineum, Yoni, Anus and Gonads

Closely followed by the Heart

Imprints traveling through the gestational fluid

Manifesting as patterns and karma in the root of existence

The primal space of the Womb (sexual organs) holding and storing generational stories and narratives to play out in matter and time

As we journey into the roots of our being we begin to awaken the layers of imprints, patterns and energy that has been locked dormant

This dormant disconnection has held our roots trapped, frozen in fear

The root chakra
The first chakra
The root of the body

Primal
Safety
Security
Physical
Body
Fear

This space holds the capacity to either connect you into the Earth's core and awaken to your primal nature OR disconnect you from your physical body and experience here on Earth.

This disconnect manifesting as a lack of safety, fear, pain, an inability to be here now, a disconnect from your body, a lack of grounding, unable to feel supported, over thinking mind energy and a lack of trust.

We heal and clear these deep rooted patterns when you journey into the Roots and soften

When we bring loving awareness to this primal space and awaken with full energy and devotion to our physical manifestation here on Earth.

Arriving at the centre point

A field of pure creation

Void of all belief

Merging into oneness

Surrendered into flow state

A point of birthing the new

Deep within us all lives a primal power

A point of light in the depths of the darkness of your womb space

Here is the place of your unlimited power

Untameable wild erotic innocence

Arriving at the Cervix

The Gateway to the Stars

Opening

Surrendering

Pulsing

Contracting

Tightening

Expanding

Dropping

Sinking

Feeling

Screaming

Waves of ecstasy

Ripples of bliss

Allowing

Spinning

Spiralling into the Abyss

Moaning

Groaning

Flowing

Sacred fluids of pleasure

Primal energy of power

Exploding

Into a million particles of light

The Cervical Gateway opening into the void of all creation

Surrender into the Rise of Shakti

Surrender into the Descent of Grace

Cervical Orgasm

Birth

Menstruation

Here you will meet the gateway of the cervix

The bridge between the worlds

The gateway to the stars

The holy grail

The sacred site of Initiation

Here you walk through the rite of passage into the exploding, life altering path of womb consciousness

Cervix of Light

The free flowing energy of the breath moves up and down the body activating and opening the cervix during birth and orgasm.

Both processes are the same energetically

The freedom of the breath flowing is a reflection of the opening to birth and orgasm.

The breath visualised as a channel of light within the landscape of the body
Moving through the central space

Heart to cervix
Naturally offers an opening of this gateway

An opening of light into birthing and orgasmic bliss as a sexual and / or birthing experience

The divine feminine

Lives within the earth

Rooted down into the Crystalline grids

She is planted in the body of Mother Earth

Awakened to the ancient wisdom of the roots

Woven within the tapestry of her soil

Codes of creation awakening

As you awaken to her

She awakens within your body

Breathe her in

Up through your root

Breathe her in

Up into your womb

Breathe her in

Up into your heart

Opening
Awakening

Expanding

Embodying her

Receive her crystalline codes of Creation

Feel the Nature of her move within you

Contraction as the path of Surrender

In states of contraction that are experienced within

Birth
Fear
Growth

There can hold an imprint of this state of contraction being painful or uncomfortable

Whether birthing a baby or journeying a rebirth of your own – both offer an experience of expansion

Expansion is followed by contraction
Contraction is followed by expansion

There can be a fear of expansion due to the inner knowing of the contraction that is essential as part of that expansive experience.

A woman may fear the contraction state of labour due to her own personal wounds and then not fully allow the expansion experience due to the knowing

the contraction will come

This can be the same within spiritual evolution

Fearing the expansion so denying the contraction needed to grow
Or fearing the contraction so never allowing and stopping expansion and
growth

Yet if we begin to unwind the imprint of contraction being a painful experience
And begin to rewire this experience as a moment of surrender
A moment to pause and soften

How would the experience be then...

With no denying of the polarity journey
Yet a welcoming of softening and surrendering into the contraction state
To be able to welcome the expansion through this point

This is the ultimate surrender into the arms of Grace
A full release of the control woven into contraction experiences
A welcoming of the state of allowance
To ride the waves and surges of life, birth and growth

The Womb Spiral

The Non Linear space

Vortex of energy

Woven
Weaving
A sacred tapestry of life experiences within

When a woman Brings awareness to her womb space she is accessing a space of non-linear energy + time.

Awakening a conscious connection to the unconscious and subconscious.

Here she may receive messages of guidance, support, wisdom through visions, pictures, emotions and memories.

This spiral space exists beyond the rational mind and invites you to drop into a release of linear expectation.
The inner language of the womb is spoken in
Thought, feeling, vibration, sensation, emotion, memory, picture, vision,

dreams, journeying, intuition and inner knowing.

An ancient wisdom that lives within the cellular memory of a thousand life times and through blood lines.

Passed down through the womb line

The spiral path is constantly inviting you to meet yourself in the waves and curves of life experience.

Awakening Earth Star Chakra

We each are a child of Mother Earth
Yet through time we have lost our earth connecting ways of life

Mother Earth calls you now to remember and reconnect to her through the Earth
Star Chakras within the soles of your feet

We journey into the roots of your body re awakening a profound connection to
the earth of your body and Mother Earth herself

Arriving at the earth gateway of your womb space
Awakening the earth star chakra portals

A beautiful awakening to Earth Consciousness

Rooted
Grounded
Earth Connection

Opening a pathway of connection between you and Mother Earth

Arriving into the womb of the earth

You are able to receive her love, support, ancient wisdom and knowledge

A feeling a safety and healing arrives as you remember you are a child of the earth

We harmonise with the primal pulse of the Earth's womb as a song of our hearts
Reclaiming our place and life on Earth

Becoming The Body of Ecstasy

Waves rise

And fall

Swirling

Spiralling

Losing all control

Let go

Release

Let go

Dancing

Dancing within the ecstasy of bliss

The body opens

Opens

To the ripples and waves

Formless

Shapes

Explosions

Awakening

The

Body

The body

Of

Ecstasy

The body

Of

Bliss

Can you allow yourself to let go

To release all holding on

Can you let yourself release

With no thought of anything at all

Can you lose yourself in the waves of life

Be taken by the spirals

Can you trust that as you lose the aspects of yourself that you once held to be true

That you are found within the release

When you fully submerge yourself

Into the unknown
Can you stay open to the knowing

That all is known here
In the nothing space

As you lose yourself

You find yourself

All aspects of your truth returning home

But you must be willing to let go

To surrender into the abyss

To give yourself to the void

To be planted

Like a seed
Into the darkness of the mother

The feminine is movement

She is everything

All at once

She is to be felt

To be moved

To move

To feel

There is no structure

No linear motion

She is the waves
The spirals
The fluctuations

Embodying the Feminine within your life is a practise of dropping the need for control or outcome

To move your body
To allow your body to be moved from within

To surrender to the landscape of your emotions

To let go into the fluctuating waves of expression

She will move through you

And take you into your deepest heart

Your wild Feminine heart

She will show you
She will take you
Until there is nothing left to make sense of
But the raw beat of her song dancing within you

Then you will know you have surrendered deeply into the ecstatic waves of her existence

When all you feel is the beat of your heart in your chest

When you feel the love of the universe melting into you

When you melt into universal love

Here within the chaos

You build a temple of love

As The Veil Thins

Both Shadow and Light
Become More Available

A deep opening up to Love
Can be the opening of the personal shadow

Love requires us to release the ego
Love asks is to let down the guard
Love shines its light into all the dark corners
Love shows what shadows are still living within

As an opening up to love arrives
An opening of the wounds
Love has a way of cracking us open
To new and deeper layers of expression

Deepening into Love

Requires a release of all that Is Not Love

The soft silent surrender

An exhale of letting go

No force
No push
No resistance

Just silence

As the heart exhales into the space of grace

No words
No thoughts
No feelings

The soft silent surrender

Into flow of existence

The soft silent surrender

Into the loving embrace trust

The soft silent surrender

Into the release of all that was once held

The soft silent surrender

A soft sigh of relief

Welcome Home

The thinning of the Veil

The opening of the gateway

The bridge between what was and
what will be

The birth canal of our current times

We are resting in between the contractions

Just as a mother birthing her baby

Mother Earth is birthing too

The cervix Gateway thinning

Ready for the passover

The veils from the other world lifting
Revealing

What is waiting on the other side

This may be the question running through your mind

Surrender now

Surrender
To the body and the breath

Relax back into the contractions

You soon will be birthed through the other side

Soften into this moment

Remembering

There is no expansion without contraction
There is no contraction without expansion

The darkness of the tunnel will soon open to the light

Surrender

Fully surrendered

Into the arms of the divine

Let Go

Letting go of all holding

Into the arms of the beloved

Release

Releasing all control

Into the space of allowing

Trust

Trusting all that comes is meant

Trusting all the leave is meant

Open

Heart expanding open

Opening into the divine frequency of Love

EACH SEPARATION AND REUNION WE
EXPERIENCE WITHIN OUR LIVES REMINDS
US OF THE UNION OF BODY AND SOUL AT
BIRTH

So My Darling

Let yourself break

Break Open

Break Free

Break Down

Break Through

Break the Walls Around Your Heart

Break the Chains

Break the Cycles

Break the Patterns

Because Where We Are Going

There Is Only Space For Love

Message from the Mother

Only when you extract the wound from the root will you create the space for the new to grow

Just like the trees planted deeply into the mothers body our ancient wounds do too

Wounds so deeply embedded within

The branches and leaves the stories and narratives played out in patterns of distorted behaviour and experiences

We can cut back the branches over and over
Which will only lead to their return

We must be willing to dig deep
Past the narrative
Past the stories
Past the now
To the beginning
To the roots

To the birth of the wound

To reveal and feel our original experiences from which all patterns and stories manifest

Only when we dig deep into the depths of our own earthly existence and experience can we find the truth

From this exploration we can feel the Original core wound of separation

The loss and grief is to be felt this deep

Deep with the cells of who we are

Only here from this place can we lift the embedded roots from the landscape of our beings

This creates a space for us to plant new seeds

To grow new life

To tenderly and lovingly nurture a new way

New growth

A new landscape

A new earth

Only when we heal the landscape of our own bodies will we be able to heal this landscape of her

It is time to dig deep into the roots of your soul

Rebirth

The void

The Primordial space of No Thing

Endless depth

Vast space

Of the Womb

Spinning

Swirling

A release of all control

No holding

No resisting

Just allowing

Let go

Let go

Let go

The energy of the vortex

Pulling you down

Drawing you in

To your limitless depths of emotions

Waves of feelings

Asking to be felt

Trapped emotions

Screaming to be heard

Years of conditioning

Dying to be seen

To be Re Born Anew

Golden Light of Creation

Awakening the golden light of Creation

Opening to a higher states of expansion

The golden light of Creation will activate and awaken ancient codes of creative consciousness held within your womb space

Your womb is your space of sacred creation

She is a portal holding your creative potential

The golden light will open this portal of Creativity

We will take a journey with the golden light to purify all that is held within the womb that no longer serves your highest point of Creation, Expansion and Abundance

Activating the womb fire
A flame of golden light

Purifying and Renewing

Releasing age old patterns and wounds held in distortion

Opening and Expanding to the golden light

To receive

Ancient golden codes of Creation

Golden templates of healing light

To awaken your womb to her natural state of creative potential

Living and Loving

With the Heart Open

The Raw Beauty of

Feeling the Deep Grief

The Awakening of

The Pure Joy

That Lives Within

The Heart

Standing Naked

Unashamed

In the Face of Vulnerability

In truth of All that is Asking to be Felt

In Service

In Devotion

To The Healing of Her

This Is the Path of Awakening to the Consciousness of Our Mother

The Awakening Path Of The Wisdom Within the Roots Of All

A space of no sound

No noise
Just Silence

Where there is nothing to be heard
Yet there is everything to be felt

The subtle currents and waves
The spirals and swirls

The sacred patterns felt as visions within the landscape of my body

The deeper the drop into this void
The more it opens up

A never ending pool of energy to be felt
An expansive experience of the breath and the body merging as one

A constant dance of
Arrival
And

Departure

A cosmic dance of

Heaven

And

Earth

A sacred dance of

Trust

And

Surrender

Sitting

Moving

Breathing

As the observer of the landscape within

The Golden Seed Planted in My Womb

A seed of possibility

Each breath breathed

Down into the depths

Of the vast space of my womb

Awaken the golden seed

Breath of life

Breathing life into this seed of manifestation

Cracking

Opening

Shoots of golden thread begin to dance

Out of the seed of light

Each thread a spiral

Each thread a wave

Weaving sacred patterns of creation

Within the landscape of my womb

The threads begin to grow

Shape shifting into snakes

Golden snakes awakening

Dancing up my spine

Swirls Of Luminous Light

Sacred patterns manifesting

Creating light codes within

The tapestry of my soul

The snakes begin to merge

And meet with my heart

Vastness arrives

As the snakes jaw opens

Blooming into a Yoni

With a thousand tender petals

Unfolding within my heart

The Luminous Light now shining

Guiding the golden snake up

Through my throat

Threads of light weaving

Meeting in my crown

Magnificent expansion

Vast space

Limitless connection

My crown opens and blooms as a flower

Geometric patterns exploding

As the thread of light waves

Into a cord of connection with the cosmic womb of the Sky

Downloads of ancient wisdom

Pouring in to the landscape of the vessel I call home

Landing within the heart space

Breathing it all down into my womb

Each breath births an opening

In the depths of this centre I create from

A new day is dawning

Fully Integrated Woman

A fully integrated woman knows her own centre
She has taken the journey of returning

She had called back all then threads of her lost soul
The threads she has placed in others
The power she has given away

She has returned home to her inner power

She moves with the waves of life
She is comfortable embodying her emotions
She embraces her many shades of seasons
She has lived in the shadows and brought them into light

She owns her story
She welcomes and allows her pain as much as her joy

She stays rooted in her centre within all her life experiences

Deep within you

There is so much more

So much more

That you deserve

So much more to be felt

Universal energy is supporting you

Constantly

Through signs

Through synchronicities

Through hopes

Through dreams

Through landing here

Through being part of this evolutionary movement

Though the inner whispers of your soul

Through the deep longing In Your heart

Feel these callings

Follow this path

Take a chance

Take a risk

Surrender and Embrace

The Magic is waiting for you

It is waiting for you
It is calling you Home Beloved

Spiralling back into the centre point

Dancing into the vortex

Entering the void

The cosmic womb

Awakening the luminous body

Weaving through the womb web of creation

You Are Here To SHINE

The Feminine is Flow

This flow state appears to look like chaos

To a mind that is stuck in resistance to the natural flow of life

Heart Womb Pulse

Drumming
Beating
Pulsing

Dancing through the waves within

Beat beat
Pulse

Ripples of pleasure
Waves of bliss

Deeper deeper
Pounding

A call within

Home come home
To the heart womb beat within

Dance wild dance
To the heart womb beat within

Pleasure awakening pleasure
To the heart womb beat within

Open vast opening
To the heart womb beat within

Soften sweet softening
To the heart womb beat within

Surrender sigh of surrendering
To the heart womb beat within

Weaving in the sacred

Our bodies and souls woven together allowing the expression of the divine through matter.

Creative spirit and sparks birthed through earthbound wisdom through our earthly beings.

It is within this weaving that we get to create and experience all senses of soul and body.

Through the weaving of spirit and matter we begin to explore our deepest heart's callings.

To feel the call of spirit

A deep yearning through the heart to be creatively expressed.

Our own unique vibration of love and wisdom that is in service to the Earth

A journey of rebirthing from heaven to earth

Wildly feminine embodiment of light

Co-creating with the stars

Dancing with magic

Spinning new realties

Weaving in dreams

Awakening the womb grids of life

Returning to the original pattern

Thread by thread

Spiralling back into the sacred centre of the cosmic womb of the universal
mother

Reborn

Messages from The Mother

You are welcome my child
You are welcome

You are safe my child
You are safe

You are Loved my child
You are Loved

You are Home here with me
You are Home

I welcome you into my arms
To soften into my embrace

You are safe here with me
I welcome you to rest upon my body

You are not to fear your power, your strength of your fullness

Journey across my sacred lands and know that these lands of my body are a
reflection of the sacredness of your own body

Hold yourself in love
Allow yourself to be all that you are

You Are Loved my Child
You Are Loved

You Are Love my child
You Are Love

The journey home
Confirming at the heart
That which the heart knows
Is already the truth
You Are Love

Sometimes

In a deep exhale

You find a sweet pause

A moment

Of clarity

A moment

Of wonder

A moment

Of seeing

A moment

Of feeling

In just a moment

Through the in and out breath

A landing

A realising

An integration of a long story

All moved in and out

Through a breath

A breath that lands all into the moment

All that may have been wrapped up in years of inner searching or years of

external running

Within that breath

An awakening

A realising

A great shift of welcoming

Landed into the body in that moment

As the body and heart sigh and exhale

You land in a space of newness

You realise

All life is experienced through the in and out breath

Descent of Grace

Grace Descends down

Upon the body

Down

Into the heart

In a moment of beauty

Grace lands through the welcoming of all parts of the self

Through love

Grace Descends

From the heavenly realm

Grace Arrives

May we rest deeply in the beloved arms of grace under the illumination of the Full Moon

A moon calling forth balance and inner harmony

May we dissolve gently all internal conflicts to bring balance to body and mind

May we awaken the inner landscape of the heart and womb as one

New Beginnings + Old Endings

As we welcome the new
We release the old

We must allow parts of us that no longer serve and that are taking up space to
dissolve

To die
To hold a funeral for them
A ceremonial space for grief
Even the parts that we wish to release

The mind holds onto them tightest
As an over identification of who we are

When we release the hold
Soften and let go of the grasp

We allow those parts their journey of death

We create space for the new to be born

Bathing In Her Holy Song

A Sacred Transmission of Love

Closing your eyes

Breathing deeply

Sinking down

Into her embrace

You are held

You are safe

You rest deeply

Softening

Surrendering

Into the waves of her sacred song

Filling

With her codes of light

Awakening

To all the beauty within you

Opening

To her ancient wisdom

Primal song of love

Healing song of light

Exploring Your Internal World

Gentle unravelings of your soul

An ancient tapestry

Woven into patterns and prints

Of Life experience passed by

An opening of space

Allowing a deeper embrace

Of all threads

Threads that create the tapestry of your life

A beautiful work of art

Stories of love
Stories of loss

Stories of joy happiness and bliss

And stories of sadness and those we miss

UnWeaving memories

Moments of time

ReWeaving threads of the tapestry of life

We Are A Reflection of Nature

She does not bloom all year round

She cycles through seasons
She dances in the change
She takes us on a Journey

Through the colours of the rainbow
She shows us the beauty
Of blooming into colour
Of releasing into darkness

She fills like a pregnant belly
So full of radiant life

She decays like a death
Revealing branches and bones

She shows us the full spectrum
Of the beauty in between

Seasons

Cycles

Nature

Flows

You are a living expression of her wonder

Allow yourself to bloom

Allow yourself to rest

Allow yourself inspiration

Allow yourself no spark of light

Give yourself to the darkness

To be born into the light

Winter Solstice

Descending Down

Down Into The Belly
Of The Earth

Down Into The Womb
Of Mother Earth

Sinking
Down
Into Her Soil

Down Into Her Womb
The Original Womb
Of Creation
Of All
Our Great Mother's Womb

Dissolving Back Into Her
Home
Returning To Her Womb
Returning To Her Love

Divine Mother's Womb

Where All Wounds Dissolve

All Separation

All Fear

Melts Away

All Illusion

Releases

Into Her Womb Of Love

Her Loving Embrace

A Returning To The Divine Mother's Womb

To Be Reborn Again

The Great Mother's Womb

Her Womb Cave of Love

Down we must journey now

Back down into her womb

Surrender

We must offer now

Ourselves into the earth

Gently we must give ourselves

Space to release

Softly we must hold ourselves

As we dissolve into the dark light

Offer we must offer ourselves

Into the divine mother's womb

The Feminine Is Not Rising

She Is Awakening

Not Rising

She Does Not Rise

She Descends

She Is Not Rising

She Does Not Need To

She Descends

And she is taking us with her

The Feminine Is Awakening

She Is Descending

Down

She Is Taking Us Down

Descending Down

Down Into The Earth

Down Into The Belly of The Earth

Down Into The Womb of The Earth

A Seed Planted

In The Soil of Her Fertile Womb

To Be Reborn New

Midwifing

Through Birth + Death

Walking the path between worlds

The mother speaks to me

My beloved child

I have taken you into the darkest places

I have left you in the deepest spaces

To show you through your own eyes

What lives between

Between each breath
Between the light and shadows
Between the worlds
Between here and there
Between life and death

Between each now
Between grief and love
Between joy and sadness

For you to see all that lives in the space between

Each Journey a deeper spiral into the transitions
of life

We must walk these paths to learn them and to know them

So we can guide others

To show them the way

To midwife them through the dark and light

To know the shadows
To know the light
To know the contractions
To know the expansions

How
Deeply
Fully
Wholly

Holy
Can we sit in the space between

The transition points of life

Where there is no thing to know

No thing to see

No thing to be

No thing to become

Hold others there she tells me

Like I taught you to hold yourself

Hold others there

Like I held you all those times

You had to be shown this

Over and over again

To know it in your body

To feel it in your soul

A great remembering

Of the path you walk between the worlds

Here through the lived experience of life and death gateways to the great
awakening open

Awakening pathways of illumination

Be the light in the shadows

Be the shadows in the light

Be the contrasts

Be everything
Be nothing

Be it all
Be nothing

Nothing can be held tightly in the space in between

Your only journey is deeper

Into surrender

Surrendering into the arms of love

My love will forever guide you here

As you midwife through the transitions of life

Birth + ReBirthing

Is A Holy Descent

We are born through a downward spiral of earthing energy

This spiral energy flows with us through our journey of life
Taking us inwards and downwards
Through each initiation
Each ReBirth

Calling forth a holy descent
Back down into your womb
Back down into the mother's womb
To be born again

Through the downward flow
Birth + ReBirthing happen through the spiral descent earth bound

We are born again

Through the Descent

Descending

Into Darkness

A calling from winter

To release down to the bones

To remember

Darkness

Is not

The absence

Of light

Darkness

Is a deep space all of its own

To be explored with wonder

And delight

Darkness

Offers velvet mystery

Darkness

Offers shimmering light

A return to darkness
Is a return to light

Darkness
Births Light

Give yourself the gift of beauty
As you surrender into the black light
Softening into the void
The space in between

Rest
Here
Rest

Allow life to pass through

Rest
Here
Rest

To be born anew

The Beginning

I Lay

Naked
Upon Her Holy Body
I Remembered
The Heavenly Beauty
Of My Body
Melting Into Hers
Humbled To My Knees
A Thousand Times
In Prayer
In Search
Of The Divine
And All This Time
She Was There
Resting Beneath Me
As An Eternal Support
Her Body
A Landscape Of Change
Constantly Teaching Me
The Art of Surrender
The Magic in New Beginnings
The Beauty of Release
Here My Body
Upon Her Body
I Found God